Happy Birthday 8th

Bristol

01/05/22

Love

Grandmom & Granddad

HAPPY

The True Story of a Stray Dog Who Became a Hero

Kate McCormick

Illustrations by Tina Ochenante

TCU Press

Fort Worth, Texas

Library of Congress Cataloging-in-Publication Data

Names: McCormick, Kate, 1965- author. | Ochenante, Christina, illustrator.
Title: Happy : the true story of a stray dog who became a hero / Kate
   McCormick ; illustrated by Christina Ochenante.
Description: Fort Worth : TCU Press, [2021] | Audience: Ages 4-10 |
   Audience: Grades 2-3 | Summary: "Who knew a street mutt could win the
   hearts of a whole town? Happy, a scruffy stray dog, becomes a beloved
   hero when a fire threatens his new home. He'll need all the help he can
   get in a town without a fire department or even fire hydrants. In this
   true story, neighbors work together to find a creative way to put out
   the fire and Happy discovers that having a friend is the best reward"--
   Provided by publisher.
Identifiers: LCCN 2021017529 | ISBN 9780875657899 (hardback)
Subjects: LCSH: Happy (Dog)--Juvenile literature. |
   Dogs--Texas--Houston--Biography--Juvenile literature. | Fire
   prevention--Texas--Houston--Juvenile literature. | Human-animal
   relationships--Juvenile literature.
Classification: LCC SF426.5 .M297 2021 | DDC 636.70092 [B]--dc23
LC record available at https://lccn.loc.gov/2021017529

Design by Rebecca A. Allen

Fort Worth, Texas 76129
To order books: 1.800.826.8911

For
Chief Mike Pack, SPFD retired
and
the late Captain Steve Cassias, SPFD

Not all homeless pets are as lucky as Happy to find a new home. That's why since 1924, the Houston SPCA has been the leading animal rescue and protection organization on the Gulf Coast. Each year, the Houston SPCA places more than 6,500 animals through adoption and 2,300 animals in foster homes, and investigates more than 6,000 cases of animal cruelty. The Houston SPCA relies solely on donations to provide this vital service. We are grateful that a portion of the proceeds from the sale of this book through 2022 will help us to continue our lifesaving work. If you'd like to learn more about the Houston SPCA, please visit www.houstonspca.org.

This is the true story of a
stray dog who became a
hero.

But on a warm day, the little dog didn't know he was going to be a hero. This wasn't his neighborhood. Or his street. And none of the houses were his home.

And he was hungry. Very hungry. The cat eating breakfast on a nearby porch never shared her food, but the little dog was skinny and scruffy, and seemed friendless.

Soon, they were sharing breakfast every morning.

As spring stretched into summer, the weather turned hot. Very hot. To keep cool, the family who lived with the cat slept with their windows open. The little dog—now named Happy—slept on the porch.

One night, soon after Happy found
his new home, he awoke with a
start. The air was thick and heavy.
He heard crackling and popping.
Was he dreaming?

No, the house next door was on fire!

Happy had to tell his new family, but how?

Happy paced back and forth, scratching at the screens on the bedroom windows. Happy scratched and he barked, and he barked and he scratched.

Finally, the family woke up. With no time to
waste, they raced next door.

Neighbors still in their pajamas also rushed to help, but they were no match for the fire. The little town had no fire trucks and no fire hydrants.

So a call went out to the nearby towns.

And they came.

One,

two,

three pumper trucks came to fight the fire!

Quickly, the firemen hooked their hoses to the pumper trucks and sprayed the fire. But the fire was too strong. One by one, each pumper truck ran out of water, and still the fire burned.

Without water, how could they fight the fire?

The swimming pool!

But the pool was far
away in the park.

The firemen knew just what to do. Working together, they joined the hoses from each pumper truck to stretch from the fire all the way to the pool.

Other firemen raced to the park in a pumper truck. They dropped a short hose in the pool and attached the long hose to the other side of the truck.

Then, they turned on the pump and like a giant straw the hose sucked the water out of the pool!

When the pool water reached the waiting firemen, they wrestled with the gushing hose.

Finally, the fire was put out, but not before the neighbor's house—and Happy's house—were badly burned.

Happy's family was sad for what the fire had taken, but they were also grateful.

Because of Happy, two families were safe.

After the fire, the people decided they needed their **own** fire department. So, they bought a shiny red pumper truck.

They put a fire hydrant on every street.

And they hung a siren on a tall pole in the park to call the volunteers for duty.

Every week the people met at the fire station to eat dinner together and to practice fire drills.

They still do. Today, they are one of the last all-volunteer fire departments near a big city.

Word spread quickly of Happy's deeds. His photo was on the front page of the newspaper.

He got a gold medal for his bravery and was later named Texas'
Greatest Dog Hero of 1931!

But the best reward was a steak dinner from his family to share with his new friend.

Photo courtesy of Kathy Bannister.

Happy was a real dog who lived in Southside Place, Texas, in 1931. Camille and Bradford Clark and their daughters adopted Happy after they found him on the porch eating their cat's food. Less than a week later, Happy woke the family in the middle of the night just in time to rescue their elderly neighbors from their burning home.

Because Southside Place had no fire department and no fire hydrants, neighboring towns were called to help. The West University Place Volunteer Fire Department and Station 16 of the Houston Fire Department sent pumper trucks and firemen to fight the fire.

When the pumper trucks ran out of water, the firemen laid over 1,100 feet of hose through the neighborhood to draft water from Southside's swimming pool. Despite these heroic efforts, both the neighbor's house and Happy's house were lost to the fire.

On June 6, 1931, the day after the fire, Happy received the prize for the most heroic dog at the first annual Houston Press–SPCA Mutt Show. Later, the Latham Foundation named Happy "Texas' Greatest Dog Hero of 1931."

Illustration courtesy of the Latham Foundation.

After the fire, the citizens of Southside Place created a volunteer fire department. They put fire hydrants on every street and hung a siren in the park to call volunteers to duty before fire calls were transmitted by radio. On December 30, 1935, Southside took delivery of its first Seagrave pumper truck.

Thirty-five years later in 1970, the pumper truck was retired from service and repurposed as a piece of play equipment in the park. Thereafter, Southside's park affectionately became known as "Fire Truck Park."

Kate McCormick lives in Houston, Texas, less than a block from where Happy became an unlikely hero in 1931. She learned about Happy while researching the history of her neighborhood for her first book, *Images of America: Southside Place*. Beginning with an undated newspaper article about a neighborhood fire, Kate tracked down the descendants of Happy's owners, who shared family photos, memories, and clippings to help bring Happy's story to life. The prepublished manuscript of *Happy* was named a finalist for the 2019 Joan Lowery Nixon Memorial Award. You can visit Kate online at www.katemccormickauthor.com.

Tina Ochenante (formerly Tina Armenante) is a children's book illustrator who studied at the Cambridge School of Art in the United Kingdom. She currently lives in San Francisco with her husband, son, and dog named Alfonso. For more information about Tina, visit www.TinaOchenante.com.